Last Thoughts Before The Exit   Cathy BLUE

Original Name: Last Thoughts Before The Exit
Original Language: English

Copyright © Tülay ASLAN. 2021

First edition, September 2021

Book design by Tülay ASLAN
Cover Photo by Tülay ASLAN

ISBN 978-605-71041-0-6

Published by Tülay ASLAN

Index

There are a bunch of people I wanna thank in this book, buckle up, this is gonna take a while. :)

My biggest thanks will go to m'twin who had always been my rock, my shelter. I love you to the moon and back. You are a blessing, always.

This special person Lindsey Armistead has given me huge inspiration while writing this book, if you have time, check over Ampersand Poetry & Prompts over Instagram and Facebook, one of the best prompt pages I had ever come across, I am proud to carry some of their lines, titles in my poetry.

I want to thank my soul family for their love, support, friendship, for always being there whenever I needed, sometimes an ear, sometimes a shoulder. I am wishing this new year/this new age will bring you all what you need, I love you all.

Last Thoughts Before The Exit

Last thoughts before the exit,
You may wanna take another route,
Ignore all the ''ugly truths'' of life.
Is your blinker on?
Can you look to the side
While someone hurts/rapes/kills
Your sister/mother/brother/father?

Delusional and ignorant we all are,
Thinking because we are secretly hoping
It won't happen to someone
We know by our hearts.

Does it matter? If we know the name?
Should it matter?
Why can't we speak out and stand out
For someone we don't know?

I will not be deaf, muted, blind.
I will write all these ugly truths out.

I will hope to make a difference,
If anything, at least it will
Be healing.

You are not alone,
We are not alone,
We were never alone,
The world is covered
With all of us.
We are all around.

Open your heart,
Open your mind,
You are not alone,
I am you,
You are me.
I love you.

Love,

Cathy

Run Morning Run

Standing in front of the bridge,
Watching a city sleep blissfully,
Only insomniacs are awake
Or workaholics, as if that is better.

The morning wind slaps my face,
My eyes tear up a little, *i-n-h-a-l-e*.
I wrap my arms around myself,
The chill is in my bones,
Nothing a wool, thick cardigan
Will manage to warm up.

I should feel grateful, to be alive,
They say, mostly knowing and
Lacking the pain to understand
What it truly means
To *s-u-r-v-i-v-e*.

I ask myself every dawn,
Did I really survive?
Am I still trying to survive?
Do I really want to survive?

Do I feel cornered to survive?

It makes me think what I am doing,
Right now, watching a soulless city
Sleeping like dead at dawn,
Standing over this bridge, close to the railway,
Proving myself I can *r-e-s-i-s-t,*
The temptation of the peace,
The temptation of game-over,
The temptation of freedom.

I don't wanna be me,
That broken, damaged girl
Standing every dawn over the bridge,
Too chicken to jump down,
Too chicken to live either.

I don't wanna be me,
Flinching from every touch,
Trying to analyze, overanalyze
Every spoken word,
Every wordless silence.

I don't wanna be me,

Shell of a human alive,
Dressing up, dolling up to work,
All rotten with worms inside.
No perfume can mask the scent of death.

I-n-h-a-l-e, e-x-h-a-l-e,
Think how far you've come,
Giving into this temptation now,
Am I that weak really?
May be because that is why
They choose you,
W-E-A-K, W-E-A-K,
Fcking *w-e-a-k.*

The fury pumps and fuels inside me,
A gasoline to the fire, I'm seething.
I push back from the bridge,
I crank my stiff neck, run back home.

Fuck them, fuck their lies,
Fuck their useless fucking system,
Fuck their justice system
Which keeps giving blowjobs to rich,
Fuck them all, fuck them all.

Fury is my friend,
Fury is all I need,
Fury understands
My need to cut open
All these old wounds,
Fury keeps my bed warm,
Fury keeps me sane.

No sir, go fuck yourself,
I do not need your worthless advices,
I do not need your blind onlooker eyes,
Fury and me, my fury in my soul,
They raped me, they raped Fury,
We are now one,
We are now molded together,
We are never alone.

They all watched the rape,
They were not alone.
Too many to blame,
Who will spill the first blood?

Blending In

Will you walk
These white halls
With me?
Will you keep shooting
These sharp daggers,
Keeping your distance?
Are you trying to prove
Others or yourself mostly
That we are not related?

What am I to you now?
A burden to drop on a fancy hospital,
Pay a hefty price, we take care of
Your human burden until you know,
We can bury it, as well,
What a gooooood riddance
For us all!

Take another step back,
·Increase the distance in worthless centimeters,
Prove your self worth to others
Just like you,
Blur all your true colors,

Blend in like a chameleon,
No backbones in your body.

RazorCut

Slay my humanity,
The world does not need
To see me weak.
Don't be shy,
Rip out all my emotions,
I had already switched them off.
Rip the band aid off of my soul.

Make me bleed,
Watch me die.
That fragile human body
Must be disposed,
Drop it on the floor to compose.

My soul is what you want,
Humans chased and lusted after
An already carved body.
My demon wants what i carved for him,
Out of my silly, naive heart.

So much blood around us,
You filled a bathtub for me, *WOW!*

Last Thoughts Before The Exit   Cathy BLUE

The rightful Queen I am,
You gently set me down
In the tube,
A different kinda Cleopatra,
I bathe in my own blood.

The lights are blurry in my vision,
The whole mundane world, a haze.
You push my hair away from my face,
Lean closer to my face, stargaze into my eyes,
Seeking the answers to the questions in your mind.

I grab you by the horns, pull closer to me,
Our lips inches away from each other,
None of us closes the gap,
We linger and hover over each other,
You exhale, I inhale you in,
I exhale you out in a sigh, you inhale us in.

Your skin gets warmer in every second,
My hands burn but I welcome the pain
You give me, it will free my soul,
It will free me, it will give me wings to fly away,
Fly away from this world.

Time Of Mind

Red footprints in the hay maze,
I have been chasing my own tail
All the while, walking on the
Shattered thin glass of my own mind.

I can't seem to find the words,
I can't seem to remember what
I was even gonna say or do,
Days, years, Months, seconds,
Everything mingles together,
Fades away like a smoke,
Only their haunting noise stays,
Echoing in my mind:
TICK TOCK, TICK TOCK.

Someone says *"Your time is up,"*
Giving me a pointing look,
Am I supposed to know or remember
What that was all about?
I try to kickstart my mind,
It shatters all the more,
I step on it, I wanna go home.

I Swear You This

I crawled my way out,
On my hands and knees,
Looking submissive,
Inwardly seething.

Not everyone has to be
Good role-models,
Some teach you
Exactly what you
Never wanna be.

I will slay my own throat,
Bathe in my own blood,
If I ever feel like
I am turning into my own mother.

Even from this distance,
Her shadow manipulates my own parenting,
Do I give in too easily?
Do I sound like her?

Last Thoughts Before The Exit   Cathy BLUE

I fear I will fail
To stop the vicious cycle
Of her mental abuse.
I promise to shoot myself in the head
Before that day comes.

Losing The Vision

Vision inside a vision,
Mind is a hectic maze,
I run to left, I run to right,
Walls up to the sky
Greet me, tall and proud.
My vision is blur, fading,
I do not know where I am,
I do not know what I am doing
Any more.

Full Of Worms

Slowly but surely,
You poisoned her soul.
Stripped her off of her confidence,
Her family, her friends….
You, a great chess player,
A narcissistic in disguise,
Sugarcoating your selfish, snob nature,
Shine that ego of yours,
Make it sparkle bright.

You played her,
Made her a muted wife,
A muted mother,
Demolished every wall
She tried to build
To shield her own sanity.

What happened in the end?
She shot herself in your
Fancy office,
Her blood stained
All your white furniture,
All your white walls,

Last Thoughts Before The Exit   Cathy BLUE

All your white floors.
It made people think,
You know,
Blindfolds came loose.

You buried her six feet deep,
Claimed she did not deserve
A lovely grave to commit
The seven deadly sins..
Her body, decomposing already,
Full of worms and various bugs.

All your circle took a step back,
Mourned her, supported her way too late.
Now, a whiskey glass in your hand,
You are standing in your fancy office,
Watching your empire crumble down
Into dust, full of worms.

Protecting Me / Protecting You

Sometimes, it is that gut feeling,
Deep in your bones,
Screaming to you to run,
Run like a damn cheetah.
But the fear looming like dark clouds,
Folding and unfolding itself,
The woohoooosshhh of your own blood
In your ears,
The echoing fastening heartbeats.
Like a deer caught in the light,
I watch the blow,
Come closer and closer to my fcking face.

I wanna get away, I wanna separate
Myself from this body,
Too late, I am paralyzed in fear.
I wanna be naive and think,
He will not hit me now,
With our baby inside me
But your slap already sends me down
To my knees and face.

My brain in auto-pilot,

Wraps my useless, shivering hands
To cover my baby,
Just in case.
You are screaming,
I can't hear,
Brain is screaming at me
To run or to kill to stay alive.

I am not as fast as you,
You grab me by the hair,
Your spits in my face,
You tug at my hair,
Still screaming in my face.
I can only wheeze,
Not even bothering to try to
Remove your hands.

You push me down,
Reminding me who is the boss.
Sobs are clogged in my throat,
I am scared you will return.

It hurts everywhere,
I can't stop the trembling,
I can't stand up,

Last Thoughts Before The Exit   Cathy BLUE

I can't mutter a sound.
I only inhale slowly,
Letting tears of embarrassment
Fall down into my belly.

I can't protect myself,
How can I ever protect you?
My mind is broken,
Cuts me deep like a broken glass.
I sit there, hands on my belly to feel you,
Watching the panic subside.

Master And Pawn In Mind Games

Hesitations of talking,
Open another drawer,
Push aside gently
Dozens of folders of
The dust-collected memories,
Sins of the omissions,
Regretted silences,
Uninspired/forced upon conversations…

You are not strong enough
To break with precedent ,
You know it, you hesitate to live,
Fake it, till you make it?

Limited days on the calendar,
Chalk up another line,
Another wasted day,
Another wasted moment
You can't take back.

How long? How long to live?
How long to truly breathe?

Last Thoughts Before The Exit   Cathy BLUE

Enough, stop it, I can't bear,
Too loud you are, too loud,
TOO FREAKING LOUD!!!!!

I can't breathe, I can't,
I can't, *gasp*, *wheeze*,
BRAIN, SHUT THE HECK UP!

Autopsy

Razorblade wet dreams I had,
Neat cuts on my pale skin.
Some healed, some stained,
They look like fading tiger stripes.

Where's your scalpel?
I read your unspoken words,
I know your hate, your small mind,
Your rotten fear of
What you can't relate to.

How sharp is your scalpel?
Where will you cut me now?
Not my face, because then
They will all see,
Somewhere private may be.

Another cut on my skin,
The pain floods inside my veins,
Blood washes away my sins,
I have far too many.

I see my veins fading,
I see your veins clearly.
I want to crack your head
To the fancy dinner table,
Crack you open,
For all you put me through.

I wanna cut you open,
I wanna stitch me alive,
I wanna stitch you dead
After holding your
Beating heart in my hands.

Come, hit me again,
I will not cower,
You are messed up in the head,
I'll fix you, I'll kill you,
I will cut you open,
I will fix you.

Making Out Of The Cage, Alive

I packed a bag for myself,
To stay in a safe place,
Away from the monster in you,
Your well-practiced lies,
''I am sorry babe,
I will not do it again,
I will break my own hands
If they are raised to you.
You know me babe,
I was drunk, I was high,
This ain't me, this ain't us,
You love me, I love you babe…''

A cold dish, heated, got cold,
Reheated, got cold, reheated, spoiled.
I swallow the bile rising,
Whenever you are drinking.
I know what is to come,
I know you will never stop
Until you make me bleed.

I make myself invisible,
I curl into a ball inside

Last Thoughts Before The Exit   Cathy BLUE

The dark closet,
Lock myself there,
Hoping you do not find me tonight,
Hoping you pass out,
Drunk on your piss and vomit.

''I am not an alcoholic,''
Another set of your lies.
I cry for the love I lost,
The more I lose it,
The more I hate you,
The more I hate myself
All along.

Endless vicious cycle,
I do not have my pride anymore,
I seek for help or
I will kill myself to make it,
To make you stop.
I am not strong enough
To make you stop.

Minutes stretch into hours,
Hours into centuries,
I piss myself in fear,

Knowing what can happen
If I am not invisible.

Tears fall down my face,
I am just numb anymore,
I won't even care if
It ends, my life, your worthless life.
I am a coward to stay,
To accept being your punching bag,
Claiming I am too brave,
Taking the blows.

I am just stupid, coward,
I do not deserve the beauty
Of the life, of the love.
Look at me, how low
I got now, rockbottom.
Is that how love is
Gonna be?
Beat you up till I kill you,
Not death tears us apart.

I hear you fall down on the floor,
Snore. I listen to it for a time,
Too afraid to move.

Last Thoughts Before The Exit   Cathy BLUE

If I do not move now,
When then? I ask myself.

A courage I fake for myself,
Untangling my sore limbs,
Walking quiet like a cat
Is an art I mastered
When you raped me once
On the kitchen floor
Cos I said no,
You were high with
Your friends.
That night, you said,
You taught a lesson
To the bitch,
Said I should be grateful
Cos you would never let
Them have their turns
With me.

I look down to you,
Drolls, vomit all over your handsome face,
A babydoll face to hid the monster inside,
A gargoyle hidden inside your gray eyes,
A monster sleeping in the lake of
Its own piss.

Last Thoughts Before The Exit   Cathy BLUE

You look helpless,
A big part of me wants to grab
The biggest knife I can find
To kill you, stab you in the heart
Like the demonic monster you are.

I have to be quiet yet again,
I hold my breath, walking out
Of the back door, I lied to you,
I did not lock it today,
May be I had learnt a few tricks
From the best.

All my fear, all my regrets,
All my wannabes, all my possibilities,
All my love/hate play dough,
All my blind and deaf hopes,
On your doorstep,
Left to the freezing night.

How Many Skeletons Can You Bury?

Unspoken words, hidden secrets,
Bottled up emotions, faked smiles,
All buried deep in your closet,
A pile growing bigger and bigger
Each and every day.

Lately, you just have to
Force the door closed,
I am installed deep in you,
You forget, I am you.

Stuff more disappointment inside,
It is getting kind of claustrophobic in here,
Layers cocoon me, layers of anxiety,
What if we fall apart?

Forcing the door closed,
What is gonna be the next step?
Installing locks? Ignoring our voices?
Your heart, beating now to break apart.

I am your pain, I am your disappointment,
I am your unspoken words,
Saying ''I am okay'' is easier.
-Another lie to bury-
I am your backbone,
I can break, bend, heal,
I am buried inside in you,
Along with these lies, pain, traumas.

We need help, you need help,
We are living only to die more
Each and every day.
We fake it, never make it.

Embrace me, embrace the pain,
Embrace everything, all these traumas,
They are ours in a twisted way.
My bones tell your story,
Your scars tell my story.

I am your leftovers,
When you die, all they will find.
We are cushioned by the meat,
Sharks try to rip it apart.

The door is come open,
May be not today, but soon,
It is just dark here, alone and crowded,
All the pain / skeletons you try to bury...

Flying High To Crash Down

Feasting on the bones of you,
I am not sad, I am only crying
Crocodile tears for the onlookers,
Who stood and watched,
Lying you to them all your life,
Eating up your sticky, sweet lies
All their lives-you can always brush
Your teeth to avoid your cavities.

I was a human like you once,
I was smiling, laughing, living,
Now I am alive to be dead
For centuries and centuries,
Eternally shackled to loneliness.

My humanity? Long gone.
It was sweet innocence of a virgin,
You chose to rape over and over,
Until you can not.
Even then, you fed me drugs,
Got me high and paralyzed,
I never survived the fall afterwards.

I wanted to survive, you broke my wings,
You tried to tame me, giving me a vampire inside,
A cold, dead, cruel, merciless, bloodthirsty vampire,
I had been dead inside for so long.

You took my faked obedience and fed it to your ego,
I grabbed a knife, I fed myself, I made fancy wall art,
I made body paint to myself, I look good in red,
Like you say, Red makes me more expensive
And easy to sell, red lipstick, your favorite,
Looks good while giving a head.

A feast you are, to my bloodthirst,
I can't get enough, I want it more,
I want to stab you more,
I see your veins clearly,
It turns me on all the more,
I want to shred you into pieces
To wipe from my existence.

My fangs look great, on your pale skin,
It makes me smile in joy, when was the last time?
How long have I been here?
I was a child once, my mother loved me,
She used to brush my hair, smell and say,

I smelt like a sunshine.

You said I smelt like a drug-addict whore,
You never appreciated your own creations,
You beat me, raped me, sold me to others,
Never caring what they did to me,
How they broke me, made me beg,
Do things I hate, to stay alive.

So you see, along the way,
This drug haze and crystal clear mind,
 I picked up some tricks, learned new skills,
I said ''Let's fly high together, have sex,''
I changed your syringe, I got you trapped
Into a paralyzed body,
Oh seee, how mesmerizing I can be…

The best part is,
Your mind was free,
It was never your body
I took down alone,
The horror in your eyes,
The tears, the stinky fear,
The pleasure is all mine.

Under Street Lights

-Inspired by the song, Here It Comes by A.J.
Music-

Comes and goes,
In waves, hits too deep,
Drags six feet down,
I can't see anywhere,
But the darkness around.

I open my mouth, sandpaper dry,
No scream, no words, nothing.
The waves come and take away
All the words, I'm buried
Into a forced, deep silence.

I wanna get in the car,
Drive for days to a brand new place,
Start over, be somebody else.
Be someone for someone,
Be someone for myself.

Car keys in hand,

Last Thoughts Before The Exit   Cathy BLUE

Feet planted in cement,
I stand there, watching the street lights,
Blink upon me.
I'm too scared to start over,
I'm too old to do this all,
I'm too young to die…

Existential crisis of mine,
Under street lights,
Always shining,
Never seeing.

Dancing In The Rooftop / Love Triangle

Tethering over the edge,
I can feel you,
You are dancing on the roof
Of a skyscraper,
One feet in, one feet out.
Flirting with both
Life and death.

You are stuck in between two worlds,
Belonging to none.
It kills you alive,
It makes you have to live,
You do not know
Where to start,
When to stop.

Keep playing the game of
Cat and mice,
Chase your own tail
In a never-ending ouroboros,
Eat your own tail,

Last Thoughts Before The Exit   Cathy BLUE

Swallow yourself whole.

You are hurting,
You are haunting me down,
I feel your pain,
I feel your anger,
I read your unspoken silence,
Your screaming deafens me.

You have always been
Restless and unsettled
In this world,
This is why you flirt
With love and death,
Playing with them both,
Not knowing which one
You really want.

Toss a white blanket
Over your forsaken soul,
Hide it from everyone,
You can't keep it
Hidden forever,
They will haunt you down.

They will never stop
Until they make you
Lose your mind in fear,
Your physical wounds
Are bleeding,
The stitches of your soul,
I see it coming undone.

They will not accept you,
You are forsaken,
You belong to nowhere,
You are different,
You are unique,
You are not part of their herd.

They will chase you away,
They will label you,
They will hate you,
They will give you a hand,
When you take it,
They will push you down,
You are already too close to the edge.

Almost in slow-motion,

Last Thoughts Before The Exit   Cathy BLUE

I watch it all.
I won't scream,
You are deaf to me,
I hold my scream inside,
Watch you jump down,
Seconds glitches into centuries,
We are stuck in that rooftop,
We are stuck in that haunting moment.

I do not hear you crash down,
It is just my damn imagination.
All these empty corridors
Of your soul,
They are all mine,
They are empty,
You are free,
You are free.
I'm stuck here.
You are free.

Cruel Thief

Take a photo,
Take a video,
Memories will fade away
In time,
Catch the moment
Before it is stolen away.

Here and there,
You'll forget so many of them,
Some of them, you will outgrow,
Memories will be there,
Feelings not.

In the quick hands of the cruel time,
Memories will dissolve and evaporate.
Take a picture, take a photo,
Remember you, remember who,
Remind you:
Who is who?

Chop Traumas Away

Chop, chop, chop,
Chop down all the pain,
It has to be in the smallest pieces,
It will not fit in the ribcage otherwise.

Chop, chop, chop,
Chin up, don't look at the blood,
Clench your teeth,
Ignore the shards of memories.

Chop, chop, chop,
Chop away the anger,
Let it go, we are
Holding onto a wrong hand
That will drag us
To the grave.

Chop, chop, chop,
Give it a break,
Let your hands rests,
A lifetime of traumas,
Won't be chopped

In one single night.

Chop, chop, chop,
Sing a happy tune,
Make it faster,
Make it all
GO AWAY.
CHOP
CHOP
CHOP!!!!!

My Remains

Suppressing so much,
Faking a smile,
Moving on,
I let them think
I am okay,
This is easier
Than trying to explain,
They will not
Understand,
Anyways.

My soul is trapped into a stone,
I always feel cold in my bones,
I fake everything I am not so much,
Always watching to be a better actor.

Night gives me a shade,
I set down my masks in the dark,
Sit by myself, talk, try to understand,
Heart of stone, I can't penetrate.

So we drink on each other's fears and pair,

We get high on the fear that is curled
Around our rib cages, squeezing the life out,
We feed it, it feeds us, a win-win business.
It comes alive like us,
When it is dark.

We fly high, we fly away,
We fear of my carved body,
It will crash and turn into dust,
Chaotic evil of mine, even you,
Will not survive.

Stars, guardians of the night
Watch us, they see the disaster unfold.
We crash down, I shatter,
Come morning breeze,
Sweep my remains away.

Walking Away

The walls are closing over me,
I'm trapped in a maze, no way out,
No way in, no rescue team, no knights.
It's just me, heartbreaks and fear.

I have to walk, who cares about no exit?
The feeling of moving ahead is better,
To stay where you are, cemented in fear.
Walk my heart, walk away, walk away.

Play Pretend

I have to hide my smile,
The big rockstar sunglasses
That cover half of my face,
Hides the happiness in my eyes.

I am good at that, you know,
Acting, play pretend.
I stand there, in front of
Your headstone,
It reads *'Beloved husband,*
Beloved father,
Will be loved, forever.'

I hold back my laughter,
My celebration drinking game
Will be seen as grieving.
People squeeze my shoulder,
Pat my back as if to say
Hey, we are here.
No, you were never there,
You just ignored everything,
Lived your ignorant happy life.

Last Thoughts Before The Exit   Cathy BLUE

I wrap my arms around kids,
We keep our silence,
Standing in front of your headstone,
We finally have peace at home.
We are finally free of your abuses.

We wait until everyone leaves,
We cry our happy tears,
Claim how we will mourn,
Love him forever,
Lie that we will miss him,
Lie that he was taken from us too early.

We go home, sit on the dinner table,
We hold hands, not to pray
But to offer gratitude,
We are finally free.
We are finally alive to live.

Boa Dancer

Like a big green boa snake,
I want to wrap myself around your body,
Gliding over your silky skin,
Wrapping myself closer,
Climbing up higher.

Squeezing your body,
Marking every inch of your skin,
It is mine now,
It is my road map,
All your skin,
I had marked.

Climb higher and higher,
Gliding over your skin
Like a blue satin sheet,
We are eye to eye,
Brown to green.

My tongue darts out
To smell and taste you,
There is no fear,

There is just acceptance,
Eagerness.

I wrap myself
Around your neck,
Squeeze it tight,
The way you like,
The way you taught.

SNAP! SNAP!
All the toxicity
You do in this life
Creates your own monsters.

I glide down,
Untangle myself,
Shift, move on.
I have no regrets
To hunt down a hunter
Who tried to hunt me down,
Who haunted me down.

Queen Of Manipulation

I sometimes feel the need to thank you,
I have been always too good
In reading inbetween the li(N)es,
I look at the sugar-coated, cotton candy lines,
See the apple rotting inside it.

I learnt how to see the truth,
Learn and master this game of
Manipulation chess.
You had always thought you won,
May be mommy dearest,
I am waiting for you to fall
At my mercy to
Take over your queendom.

People say I am a force of nature,
All I see is a destructive storm,
Fury and too much rage,
I know I can't stop
If I start once.
I'm good at suppressing
It all down,
Without beating anyone.

So you see,
As you still think
You have the upper hand
Of a backstabber,
I only play
Weak and coy deer to you,
Luring you into my own trap,
Making you lower your guards down,
Be vulnerable and unprepared
For the last strike you
Never expect.

Oh, Mummy dearest,
Beat you up
In this manipulation game
Of daughter and mother,
Forced by blood,
Nothing more,
Nothing less.

Never fall on my mercy,
I was taught better than
Showing mercy to an enemy.

Chasing The Light

-Inspired by the song, Fireflies by Yourgirlmusic-

You need the darkness,
You wrap it around yourself
Like a superhero cape.
You cling to it,
Unable to let it go.
It's too tight,
It's too suffocating,
It's choking you down.
I'm watching the disaster
Unfold slowly.

You, wrapping the darkness
Around your neck tighter
So it stays put
While you are chasing
Behind the light
You had lost.

Feral Stray Cat

-Inspired by the song, Purple by Yourgirlmusic-

I don't have the guts,
To take the hand you offer.
Many used it to pull me down.
I'm now like a stray, wild cat,
Ferrous, always hissing and clawing
In utter fear.

I don't believe that
You'll love me,
I can't lower my guard down,
I can't trust anyone.
I had repeated this mistake
Oh, so many times before.

Don't hide the disappointment,
I see it in the dark, clearly.
Paint me a villain,
Paint me emotionally unavailable,
Paint me a coward,
Paint me purple,
Paint me in new bruises,
In the name of love

For guiding what was
Broken beyond repair
So many times before….

Putting A Lipstick On Depression

They look at me,
At my perfectly well practiced make-up,
At my clean and crispy clothes,
They wonder why I feel the way I do,
They judge me with their gazes,
How can you still be depressed,
You have everything you want in your life!!!!!

I can't say my side of story,
They will not believe me,
They will play it out, twist it,
Until I am the *awww, poor sensitive one.*

I swallow down everything,
Watching the depression grow stronger in my soul.
I put on make-up, I put on a good show.
One day, it will swallow me whole.

High To Live

I told her the truth,
She never believed in me.
I had no reason to lie,
Not to her, not now, not then.

He played it off,
He said i misunderstood
The dollhouse game.
He said that kids had
Crazy imaginations.
I did not imagine anything,
He washed all the proofs.

She never wondered
Why I woke up screaming
In the middle of the night,
Why I flinched from every touch.
He said it was a phase,
He said I was afraid of
The boogeyman tale he read to me.
He was the boogeyman,
He did not tell you.

Last Thoughts Before The Exit   Cathy BLUE

He caught me hiding
My ripped and dirty underwears
To show to you,
He grabbed a fistful of hair,
Ripped it, smashed my head to the wall,
Where it would not leave
An easy-to-see bruise.

I begged him to stop,
He slapped me, said,
If I did not give in to him,
He would hurt you,
Make me watch it.
I took it all, for you, mom.

You never believed me,
You said I was just jealous,
You were happy.
I became more silent,
More distant,
You never cared.

Until I recorded it,
Went into a police station,

Last Thoughts Before The Exit   Cathy BLUE

Played the video in the public,
I had never seen police move so fast.
They asked a lot of questions,
I had proof, they all watched my proof.
Their faces grew red with anger,
They tried to hide their anger,
I was broken and scared because.

I told them that I can not go home,
You would not believe what you would watch,
You would make excuses,
A child can lure a man to her bed?

They called social services,
They deleted everything
Showing I had lived once.
They gave me a name,
They gave me a house,
They helped me to be someone.

I became someone high,
I became someone they hated,
They knew why, they still helped.

Last Thoughts Before The Exit   Cathy BLUE

I need my drugs,
My body is the only way to earn my share,
It had never been mine,
It had always belonged to someone else.

I need my drugs,
I need to numb this pain to breath,
I need to silence this train of thoughts,
I am not a child anymore,
Yet I have never been
Sleeping peacefully….
No more...

No Shelter To Hide

Do not beat me mummy,
I am a kid, I only played.
Do not beat me mummy,
I did not mean to make
My new dress dirty.
Do not beat me mummy,
I will not tell daddy.
Do not beat me mummy,
You are scaring me,
Do not hit me,
The hate in your eyes
Hurts more than the blow.
Do not beat me mummy,
Do not, do not.

But you did not stop,
You never stopped,
When you could not
Get physical,
You hit my mind and soul.
You always beat me up.

I was a girl once,

Last Thoughts Before The Exit   Cathy BLUE

I needed the unconditional love
Of a loving, caring mother.
You threw me the wolves,
Let them take a piece,
Turned blind and deaf,
For all you care.

I was a girl once,
Now I do not know
What I am,
So much fury and hate,
Building stronger every day.
Waiting for the day,
You will fall on my mercy,
And you will,
I have always been the strongest
In the family,
How ironic is that now?

Read my words,
You will fall, on my mercy,
Down to your knees,
I am getting stronger,
You are getting older, weaker.
The question is only when?

Mark my words,
You were never
Able to break me.
I will break you all over,
Every damn inch of
Your venomous soul.

Rolling', Rollin'

It keeps building and building,
This tension on my chest,
Like a rattlesnake,
Shaking its tail in warning,
Flickering its tongue out
To taste my fears,
I am paralyzed in horror,
Watching in get bigger
Every day.

Some day, I do not
Wanna get out of the bed,
I wanna sleep the day away,
Brain is full of dangerous thoughts,
Wanna unplug it and sleep in peace.

I watch it only, paralyzed in fear,
Can't scream, it is useless,
It will swallow me whole,
It won't even chew me,
Depression is rolling and rolling
Like a damn avalanche,
Ready to tackle me down,

Bury me down,
I stand no chance.

Unborn

I embrace everything
I was given,
They took too much,
I have to keep what's mine.

I hear it in the wind,
The time is coming.
I smell it in the wind,
Your body is already
Decomposing alive.

I am hosting a party
To celebrate all
Small victories of mine,
Toasting to a body
Which is too late to die.

I have been a mother,
I have been a soul sister,
I have been a soul auntie,
I have never been a daughter.

Gravedigger

I am a poet,
I am good with words,
I know how to read inbetween the lines,
I know how to decorate in between my lines.

I know what you will see
When you read my poetry,
I am the God, I am the Creator,
I am a perfectionist by my nature,
I will say, I did not leave
Any openings or clues for you.

I shut tight all the windows and doors,
I put glitters on my soul where
Claws of anxiety reached.
I decorated them in funky glitters,
You see my sparkling allure,
Drawn to it like a fly in a trap.

I buried so many words, pain,
Anger, disappointments, self doubts,
Self guilts, more anger, all fading
In the background of my soul.

Last Thoughts Before The Exit   Cathy BLUE

I buried you all along with them,
My childhood, I kissed you good night,
Sang you a lullaby, tucked you in,
Safe and sound.
In Between my closets, full of corpses.
Rip baby. Rip. Rip.

Shot To Reborn

Pulled the trigger too slowly,
In slow motion I watched
The smoke lick the air,
The silver bullet pierce my soul.

Here and there, left its hints,
I was too naive and blind to notice,
I paid the price, I took the hit,
Went down on my knees,
Pulled the trigger too slowly.

She looked at me in the eye,
Reminded me of what I was before,
What I had always been for her,
Who I had to be, for her, for her big plans.

Denial is the lie we want to cling to,
It is easier, keeps sanity intact.
I tried to deny, I tried to suppress,
She tricked me into her own magick,
Cast a spell on me, I call it a curse.

She did not care, she wanted me
For the restless, roaring beast I am,
For the fury of storm I carry inside,
She put me a damn leash,
Tied me down like a damn dog.
She looked me straight in the eye,
I watched lifetimes fade in front of my eyes,
She fcking pulled the trigger so damn slowly...

Staking The Toxic

Feed on my blood,
Cut my veins open one by one,
Lash out, rip them open,
A crimson smell so deadly.
Let it fill the air between us.
Breathe my blood,
Fill your lungs,
I know you want a taste of me.

Your tongue licks your lips hungrily,
I do not have to imagine the salvia
Pooling in your mouth,
Your eyes eat me alive,
Your eyes stab me alive,
You are afraid to take a bite,
A sip of what I am offering.

Difference between you and me,
I never backed down from a challenge.
Failed sometimes but never backed down.
Now, read this verse very carefully,
I stitched it raw and all smilies,
You will never see the catastrophe,

Last Thoughts Before The Exit   Cathy BLUE

I hid it very well in between my lines.

I am always lurking on the back of your mind,
Hearing every unspoken thought,
Every lashing out you manage to stop,
Between your clenched teeth.
Yet, you hate it in the dark,
This is why you try to drain me alive,
For the comfort I provide,
For the light I bring to your miserable life.

You, nothing but a toxic, narcissist, manipulator,
Hiding and cowering behind the lies,
Trying to play chess with your God,
Forgetting how I foresee all the moves you do
Before you move.

I am just sorry for you,
You will die alone.
I always thought I would
Stand on your damn grave,
Now, I think even your death
Is not worth wasting my time,
Emphasis on WASTING.

You, a fcking vampire, hungering
For blood and light,
Afraid of both, can't have both,
Throwing adult tantrums all around,
'Cos you never had the guts….
Lashing out, trying to destroy
Every beautiful thing in life,
Stomping your feet to
Make an impact on your miserable life,
I am the wave that washes it all away.

You tried so hard but with
This poem, I am burying you
Back to the graveyard,
Breaking your toxic chains
-You never got a hold of them anyways-
I stand over your rotten egg of a soul,
Stab it, stake your soul, slay it down,
Millions of pieces of venom
Spreading all around.
But hey, now and here,
It ends with me.

The Last Episode

My throat was burning,
Swallowing all these unsaid words,
Shards of anger, cutting down all my insides.
I washed it all down,
Kept the iron fist control over my tears.
They leaked inside,
Flooding my heart.
Nothing I can not handle.

Talking not to be listened,
Talking to be belittled,
Talking to be labeled,
Talking to be ignored,
I do not know why
I even bother….
Never worth the breath,
Time I spend.
Always backfiring.

You, hating my silence,
When I let my eyes speak,
Muting my words.
How uncomfortable you get,

Last Thoughts Before The Exit   Cathy BLUE

How angry you feel
Not being able to
Start a fight over nothing.

I let my silence
Linger in the air,
Giving you a stone wall
To deal with,
You can use it as a crying wall,
When the times comes,
When you can't handle it
Any more.

I do not care, you know,
You see it the way
I am gazing at you,
Flinching away from your touch.
You know, I am full of fury and hate,
You know when you fall at my feet,
I will walk over you and damn,
The world will continue to spin.

Blank Page

Boney hands of time,
Clinging on me,
Trying to rip it all out,
Memories, moments, songs,
Books, movies, lyrics,
Melodies, smiles, tears,
Details of our lives….

Time throws a crips, white linen
Over our memory,
Cutting the connection to
All these small details we carry
With us, what makes our life
A well lived life.

Like a damn blank page,
It is all erased, blank,
Nothing left to remember
Who you were,
Nothing left to remind you
Who you were.

Time erased it all,
Time erased us,
Time erased me,
Time erased you.
Who?

Howling

In front of a bonfire,
Warm and cozy,
We all sit together,
As a big, happy family.

We understand each other,
We get on well,
We respect each other,
We have trust on ourselves,
To the bond we have.

We hunt down together,
We kill together,
I cook, we eat together,
Sometimes we eat
All the pain raw,
Uncooked, not-seasoned.

Sitting under the stars,
I let them lick my wounds,
Wolves of worry,
We are a big clan,

I feed them, they feast on me,
They feed me, they lick my wounds clean,
They lead, I follow,
Wherever we go,
Blood follows,
A crimson river for us only,
We bathe in my blood,
We stitch me back,
For tomorrow,
For the next day,
For another day.

Howl my broken soul,
HOWL!

Captain Leaves The Ship As Last

Trying to find my own footing
On a ship in a storm,
Sliding here and there,
The ground is slippery,
Nothing to grab,
Nothing to hold onto,
It is just me,
Versus the waves
Making the ground more slippery.

Bravery does not matter,
You can not hold onto it,
It does not balance your core,
I am unbalanced,
I have nothing to hold onto.

The ground is slippery,
I open my arms wide,
Doing a weird bird dance
For balance.
It's useless,
Trying to grasp onto
What is not even there.

The waves keep coming,
Never met another soul
More restless than I,
Me versus these waves,
They have the upper hand.

I do not wanna fight
In a war to lose,
I am not cut to lose,
I am losing it,
The ground is shifting
Under my feet,
The ship is sinking,
My mouth is full of water,
I can not breathe,
I can not breathe,
I can't,
I can't,
I won't...

Sharing souls

We are all connected,
Over our words, our arts,
Our beautiful fragile hearts.
Our souls are together
In this game of life,
Against universe,
We are stronger together,
We are gonna lift up each other.

Life changes, circumstances never stays
The same, the ground keeps shifting.
Yet, hear my promise,
A part of soul will always be with you,
No matter what happens,
For this rebel part of my soul was
Never mine to keep.
I love you, take care of me.

Restless Tides

Grief,
Does not run on clock,
Does not have a timeline
Or a finish line.
It comes and goes
In strong waves,
Trying to take you under.

It is not a straight highline
Where you go full speed,
It sometimes drive you in full speed,
Nobody has the chance to buckle up,
It hits the brakes too hard,
You watch yourself, flying
Out of the window,
To crash down, hard, to the asphalt.

I can't take away your pain,
I can hold your hand,
Offer my shoulder and ear.
A silent break between the tides,
Nothing less,
Nothing more.

Die To Feel Alive

Let it strike on me,
Let the lightning charge,
Strike me over and over,
Again and again.
I will take all of it,
I will bear the pain,
There is a beauty to it,
Being broken beyond repair.

Come, I dare you,
Heavens of hell,
Let it out,
Lightning strikes twice,
Never gonna be enough,
Let it strike again.
Can't hurt more than this,
My hands are cut,
My fingers I can not see,
Just too much blood, too much blood.

I want it numb,
I want to hover over the bridge,
Watch it in the silence of dead.

I want to hang myself,
Watch my soul wiggle and dangle,
A broken doll.

Pieces of me has shattered,
Somewhere along the way,
I expired, my time was up,
This is me,
Living to die every day,
I laugh at the ones
Who are afraid to die.

I want to jump over the bridge,
Let me feel alive before I die.
I want to cut myself into pieces,
Let me make the pain bleed out.
I want to strangle myself like a hangman,
Let me look good for once before I go.

Look in the fucking mirror,
That is not me, that is not you,
That is death wearing my face,
That is death wearing my face,
You ask me stupid questions,
But there is nothing more.

Disorientation

I do not remember her anymore,
The girl before all of these,
She is dead and gone,
I see her ghost sometimes.

She is lost in the sands of time,
Whirlwind of memories,
I do not know who you are,
Not anymore...

Shoulder / Ear

Dig yourself a grave,
Get in, move aside, let me,
I will stay near you.

We all have regrets,
Some days we really live,
Sometimes we pretend.

Find a shoulder, ear,
Keep swimming to the shore, live,
Grief, regret, love, hope.

I Will Always Love You

Flashback me in time,
When my younger self
Would not even dream about
The things I had achieved.

She had a beautiful heart,
A naive one, always hoping,
Always trying to see the best
In the worst people.

She was stuffed in a cocoon,
Prisoned, ordered to stay there,
Pressure around her, lashing outs,
She was caged down like a wild animal.

So she had to be one, to stay alive.
She ate up the lashing outs and spit back
To their hypocrite faces,
She stayed in the cocoon.

She slayed her own heart, burnt it alive,

The cold ashes of it made a great steel armor,
She shaped them into scales,
Fit snugly over her skin.

She slayed these toxic ties,
Slayed anyone who tried to hold her back.
She had always been a black sheep,
She evolved into something more, stronger.

Monster, she was named,
She settled for the demon,
It fit better to the endless
Fury and hatred she was given,
It suits her more.

I am proud of you my love,
For making it alive out of the cage,
Giving me these beautiful scales,
They can never penetrate our skin now.

Wash Me Grief, Bury Me Along

I carry your heart with me,
I tried so hard to stop,
I do not know how to stop.
Waves of grief pull me under,
I hold my last breath, goodbye love.

Golden Smile

A warm smile is what you see,
When you look at me,
My expensive, neat clothes,
My picture-perfected make-up,
I am the Goddess of allure.

I am the best actress you can see,
I am good at deep swallowing
All the harsh words, belittling sessions,
I am good at hiding all the bruises
Of my body, my soul,
Purple, black, blue, pink, orange,
All the hues in between.

They'll never believe me,
They all are blinded by the dazzle
Of a multi-dollar worth mansion,
Faking to care husband,
Monster in hand-sew suit.
My unspoken words and me,
We fade into each other more.

Last Thoughts Before The Exit   Cathy BLUE

I am a trophy wife,
His beautiful doll and hand bag,
To carry around, to show off.
I am made of crocodile skin,
All my tears had to be crocodile tears,
Nobody will believe in me anyways.

Born to die in a white picket purgatory,
A golden mask I carry,
A golden smile,
A shattered heart,
A broken soul,
Golden necklace and earrings
On my never beaten face,
I wait to die,
I can't wait to die.

Break My Curse

I want to release all that tension
I have been dragging around,
I want to take you high, throw down,
Show you the beauty of being the fallen.

It is not only you who has fallen,
I had fallen from my own kingdom,
I am forsaken from heaven,
I am a refugee, running around unleashed,
I have no home, just empty houses,
I have a roof over my head,
Yet no safe place to rest.

I ripped my own wings,
It is good for soul to cut down toxic ties,
These come in many shapes, disguises.
I saw it, I cut all out.
I bled, stitched myself alive.
I cut my body to keep soul intact.
Tough choices we make every single day.

With or without wings,

Last Thoughts Before The Exit   Cathy BLUE

I can't fly anymore,
I am spellbound,
I am summoned, always,
I am lured out,
Baited.

Here and there,
Inside your mind,
Inside your body,
Inside your soul.
No homes, no wings.
I am anchored
To earth
By gravity.

Every circle has to complete itself,
Every loop has to circle back to itself,
Kill me, set me free,
Too late to love me,
We have to lose,
You have to slay me,
Do not hesitate,
Do me a favor:
Break my curse.

Let The Pain Flow Through

Screaming my heart out, so loud,
I am muting life with the remote,
Can't deal with it now.

Stop talking inside my head,
The tears that fall from my eyes
Are not mine, I do not own them,
They are unloved, unwanted,
Just like me, just like you.
Yet now I am crying the hate
In anguish, I need it out.

Let it out, let it flow through,
These emotions of yours
They do not flow through me,
They fulfill me even after
I am leaking,
I am clogged,
These emotions come in waves,
Nonstop.

Has it been some kind of race?

Last Thoughts Before The Exit   Cathy BLUE

A challenge perhaps?
To see how much I can take?
Are you looking for my breaking point?
Good luck with that,
I lack of it.

Being the warrior I am,
I am cleaning the blood
From my armor and face,
I am embracing my inner tornado.
I lay down my sword,
Open myself, come, cut through me,
No hesitation, no fear, no second thoughts,
Cut through my mind,
Cut right into my soul.

Stab me to sleep,
Burn me a sage, cleanse my dirty soul.

Sage scented dreams,
I am here, I am there,
I am nowhere,
I am everywhere all at once.
Thorns prickle my blood at every step,
But again,

Last Thoughts Before The Exit   Cathy BLUE

There is no rose without a thorn.

Little pain to endure,
Let it flow through,
Let it flow through,
Embrace your inner tornado,
Embrace your inner warrior,
Grit your teeth, breathe,
Let it flow through...

Ouroboros

One of these days,
Rain, wind, wild, strong,
Soothing my demons.

A cup of coffee,
I see all the future,
All the memories,
Through my blindfold,
Merging together,
Bleeding into each other.

The circle is broken,
We can not fix it.
It will tear us apart,
It will be our end,
Ouroboros of my soul.

Bloating

Knowing the fact that sugar is bad for your health,
Does it stop you craving candy, sweets?
Do you ignore the simple fact and playing ignorant
To satisfy your sweet tooth?

This is me, this is you, this is our life now,
We are toxic to each other, we are not healthy,
I ruin you for everyone including me and you,
You cling to me worse than a baby,
Always seeking my attention, my silent confirmation.

I ruin you, I challenge you out of your comfort zone,
I push you down the cliff and leave you wondering
If I will break the fall or just let you fall this time,
Yet, here you are, here I am, still, here.

You are holding me too tight, suffocating,
Most days, I am unable to breathe,
Most days, I want to punch the walls,
Choke you down, slay your tongue,
You talk simply too much, too much.

We are toxic together, mismatched pieces
Of the puzzle,
Somehow we fit together,
A dark, twisted way.
Obviously not everything in life
Is supposed to make sense.

Somethings we see, hear, touch, taste, smell,
Without any reality for the brain to grasp.
Let it try to sort its way out of the shit it's buried in,
You are here, I am here, we are feeding each other
With too much candy, I am high on the sugar,
Yet oh boy, do I still crave for more?

You know, not always age brings wisdom,
Sometimes it is just you fighting with your self,
You know you should've known better,
You know you could've done better,
You know you would've done better,
Yet here I am, guzzling down
All your toxic sweetness
Like a hungry wolf.

Cinderella

Sweetie, take off your comfy sneakers,
Here, wear these shards of glass slippers,
Let them cut you in every step you take,
How much pain, will you be able to endure?

Criticizing and belittling is always fun, no?
Does it make you feel stronger? Better?
Does it feed your venomous ego?
The snake is circling around your chest,
Sweetie, are you able to breathe?

Let's switch places now,
Since you think my life was easy,
You assume I was born with a golden spoon.
I assure you, it was not even close.
But again, you will never believe,
We have to do it the hard way.

Wear my glass slippers, open me your mind,
Let me trap you in so you have the first row seat
To all the pain, anger, disappointments,
Traumas over traumas.

No sweetie, hush hush,
We can't give a break, we just got started.

Why trying to cover your eyes, sweetie?
Don't like what you see?
What did you expect to see?
This loneliness, this pain, this fury…
Ahhhh sweetie, is it too much for you?

But wait, that is not how it ends,
We are not in half yet!!!!!
Are you crying sweetie?
Are you crying your own tears or mine?
Are you confused, sweetie?
You sound a bit lost, trapped inside my mind.

STOP YOUR WORTHLESS CRYING!
Up on your feet now!
You chose to abuse, now we are taking turns!
Walk a mile in my bloody shoes,
Every step you will take will cut deeper,
You won't feel numb, nope, not yet.

We do not welcome tears here,

Last Thoughts Before The Exit   Cathy BLUE

Crocodile tears these are, worthless and fake
Cos you only cry when it is you who is hurting,
Walk a mile in my shoes, let it cut your soul apart,
Let it break your skin, let it teach you a hard lesson,
Never try to bully, never try to underestimate others.

Walk a mile in my shoes, bleed for me,
Bleed for all of us.
Your time has come.
Ticking bomb.

BOOOM!

Leakage

This fragile human body
Can not contain
Me and my demons
Any more.

I have to break through,
I have to discard it,
Die to reborn,
My soul is leaking out of the pores.

Deer, Trapped

My soul is a thunderstorm,
Pain echoes and roars inside my brain,
Flashes of worthless memories
Lit up my consciousness.
I stand still, deer caught in the headlights,
Breathe, let the lightning light your way,
Breathe, let the thunder tell you your forgotten tales.

Caged / Trapped

I am starving, I am about to die of hunger.
There sits a fresh piece of cheese on a rat trap,
I see the cheese, I see the trap,
I feel the hunger, I read the desperation,
What choice do I really have
To risk a bite and hope to slay alive?
I am gonna die in both ways.

It is what it is,
What is written can never be erased,
Deleted, reserved.

RIP my soul, RIP.

MAY DAY

Give it a shake,
Watch the glitters float inside,
Rain down, all sparks.
It makes you smile,
It makes you happy,
It makes you feel carefree.

I am the one
Stuck in a snowglobe,
My world is this,
It does not change,
It is the same every day,
It is the same old, same old story.

There is too much water,
There is too much glitter
To hide the depression,
Leaking from the corner.

Ignore it, you do not care
About what I feel, go through.
I look at my best, always,

Last Thoughts Before The Exit   Cathy BLUE

Here, let me refresh my makeup,
Fix my hair quickly.

Go ahead my once-a-friend,
Give it a shake,
Let the glitters rain
All over my depression.
Again, I repeat,
Nothing I can't handle….

Pass Me The Popcorn

Sit back, watch the shit show love,
We got front seats, we got pop corn,
Watch them blow out all their furious fire,
Watch them swallow all their harsh words,
Watch them make us laugh, while they are dieing inside,
Watch them train animals cos we all know,
How hard it is impossible to train humans.

Here, love, take a handful of popcorn,
Stuff it in your mouth, you can never
Scream out loud when your mouth is full.
You are welcome for the tip.

Sooooo love, enjoying the shit show?
My mind is a freaking circus,
Up is down, down is up,
Right is wrong, wrong is right,
Every surface is a slippery ground.

Did you not see the applause and laugh warning?
It had been flashing inside our eyes for a time by now,
While we watch my life rolling into a whirlwind,

Turning into a big freak show.
Damn, this gotta be good, pass me the popcorn.

Stress-Smoker

Lit a cigarette for me love,
Inhale all the poison for us,
I see you through the veil of smoke,
I see your clearly,
Clenching your teeth,
Keeping the smoke inside your soul,
Letting the poison go as deep as it gets,
Like all our broken dreams.
Let it all go down the rabbit hole,
Destroy the heart, kill the soul.
Not all dreams are meant to be alive.
Snub them out, love.

Bang Bang

Standing tall, dead and numb inside,
Watching my own funeral,
Watching all the crocodile tears they shed,
Watching them all speak gibberish,
Oh how they loved me,
Oh how they loved me!!!!

I am now free to do as I please,
Play all games by my own rules,
Cry me a river, cry me an ocean,
Let me swim, I wanna skinny dip.

Love, you are the terrorist of my heart,
Hope, you are the terrorist of my heart,
I won't poison my soul anymore,
Mind, lead my way, I'll follow,
Bang bang, I shot my baby down!

Donation Check

I always wanted to live like that,
Blind, deaf and mute,
Crazy happy in my ignorant world.
Nothing can burst my happiness bubble.

Who cares if people are dead? Raped?
Starved to death? Murdered?
There is too much of us in the world,
Anyways.

What hue of pink should I paint my nails today?
Ballet slipper? Flamingo? Cherry blossom?
Hollywood Cerise? Barbie pink? Razzle Dazzle Rose?

What designer should I wear today?
Where should I take my selfies?
On our luxury yacht? Mansion?

Take my happy picture,
Let me dazzle millions,
I had always wanted to live like that.

Who cared about poor, anyway?
Let me sign you a donation check.

Shark In A Zoo

Do not glare at me, you do not know me,
I am just a shark forced to swim in shallow pools,
I do not have enough space to circle,
All circles lead back to me.

They trapped me here,
Giving me food and water when necessary,
Never knew love or care,
But I am very familiar with domestic violence.

My tongue is cut, they have it,
They had framed it for you all to see.
I am silent and muted,
The tornado of emotions I have is not.
It seeps from my half-dead, glassy eyes,
It reinforces pity on you onlookers,
Never shame, never take the blame
To play your part.

They have to put me down soon,
The latest news will claim on
A dramatic cut on the funds,

Their budget is limited to keep me alive.

There is nothing else you can do,
Other than playing your part
In all of these games.
They agreed to pay compensation without prejudice,
I do not care about you onlookers,
Sell your rotten souls to demons.

Swimming In Cold Water

I cry for so much and for so little,
For the little moments we had missed,
Time had moved on, we stood still,
For these big chances we had missed,
Because we were either too scared
To take the leap of the faith
Or simply too proud to be
The first one to take the first step.

Nobody can and will bring back the time,
We can not stop the flow of a river,
We have to keep swimming to the shore,
Shhhhh, let the river take away our tears,
It will cleanse us, it will drown us
In the cold water of time.

That Fateful Evening

You came home, fuming.
We all walked on eggshells,
Well-knowing how loud they
Would/Could crack.

My voice became low,
I found excuses,
Feeding already-fed kids
So they stayed out,
Out of your way.

Your tension echoed,
Roared inside the house.
Plaster a trembling smile to my face,
"Why don't we play
With the toys in your room?
Why don't we read a book?
We can do painting?"

All the ideas of some
Quiet-time, invisible time.
I ushered the kids out of your way,
Kept busy, fed, bathed, read to sleep.

I have no fear for myself,
I know you will beat me again,
I will heal, I always heal,
Don't I, honey?

The scars run too deep,
Their purulence poisons
My once beautiful soul.
I am full of venom, hate, fury,
Switching between.

Try me now,
I am overflowing with venom,
I want to be the one
To spill warm blood,
Lick it off my face.

Lay a hand again on my kids,
Try me now,
You do not know how
But I will kill you.
Without blinking,
In cold blood,
No second thoughts,
No hesitations,
No mercy.

Diamonds

Dazzling, mesmerizing diamonds shining
On my fragile human body,
Show the world how we took the hit,
How we survived, how we did it
Over and over again.
Show off our strength to the world,
My scars, the crown I carry.
This world is not gonna bring us down.

Keep Swimming

We are one, we are different,
Yet we are the same.
We stand under the sky,
We stand on the earth,
We all wish for love and peace.

Fighting to find our way back home,
Swimming through the tides of time,
Find me, find you.
I love you.

Dirty Little Secrets

I sat down, wrote,
Stitched my scars back,
Fixed my armor,
Cleaned dirt and blood from my scales,
I healed myself every day,
Ready and strong for a fight, always.

Then to heal my shattered soul,
I wrote and wrote,
It had always been the ones
I kept to myself for you,
That had cut deepest.

Curse Of Soulmates

One lifetime sooner, one lifetime later,
We are destined to together, somehow,
I will let the universe sort out *someway*.

Time is frozen between our souls,
Our magnetic pull erases the distances.
I remember it, comes back in pieces.

We stood under a big tree, facing each other,
I put my hand over your heart, I promised,
I won't leave you to die alone love,
Not in this lifetime, not in others.

Close your eyes, open your mind,
Remember who we were, remember what we are,
Before you cause us to die all alone,
Before it is too late.

I'm too tired to live to die.

Pacing And Waiting

We have nowhere to go,
We are stuck in the cage of the time.
We are prisoners of our own rational minds,
We seek what we refuse to see.

Sooner or later, we have to find
The road that leads back home.
I have been waiting for you,
Pacing inside an empty, old house,
Silly, naive heart,
Hope always remains.

PowerPoint Slides

It feels like I am dead
Or in the process of it,
Watching my life flash
In front of my life.

Powerpoint slides that is,
Add shape, music, comment,
Make it look fancy, alluring,
We all know: it is just boring!

Tell Me The Time

Teach me how to tell the time,
How to measure it.
Seconds stretch into days,
Minutes disappear inside months,
I am constantly confused,
Trying to swim, keep my head up,
Above the water.
Tell me, when will this end?

End Of A Marriage

Has it all been my mistake?
Will you blame me for it all?
Are you gonna man up,
Accept your part in the fall?

I had seen the end in the beginning,
From the beginning to the end,
I just watched, all the games
You tried to create and play.

I wish I was not numb towards you,
Anger, hurt, disappointment, hate….
I have none of these,
Just relief that it is all over.

Sky Tall Walls

You are addicted to the safety I had provided,
Thinking you can come and go as you please,
Forgetting you can't take love without giving it at first.
Suppressing and letting it flow in between,
A new trick I had mastered last week.

I do not welcome you anymore in to my mind,
Sky tall walls for you, I've been building,
My mind is a construction site, full in action,
Yet there you are, another onlooker,
Watching and wondering and hoping if I will feel again,
Knowing I will feel again without you.

I guess every good thing in time
Comes to an end.
This is it. Our end.

Drive Away My Heart

We have no destination,
I have no we, it is just me,
Driving, sipping my coffee,
Writing to heal, breathe,
Passing the streets in blur,
Leaving crumbles of breads
To the lane of lost memories-
I have no intention to return.

Wishing Well

There is a crack on the wall,
All the pain keeps leaking out,
In small doses, drip, drip, drip.
The noise irritates me, drives me crazy,
It does not stop, I want silence,
The pain keeps leaking,
Drip, drip, drip,
Into the pit of my broken soul.

Self-Destruct

Cut me open, slay me, mark me,
Break me as much as you want,
Hold tight, suffocate, cling to me,
Kill me, throw me down from the abyss,
Drive me to the walls, crash us, no air bags,
We were never supposed to survive,
Do not ask me now, what is love..

Friendship

I can't do this all alone,
I need you to walk with me.
Some days I need you to be an ear,
Some days, be a shoulder and let me cry it all out.
I want to stay sane, help me out.
Do not shut me out, do not leave me behind,
Take a step to me and I promise to take more,
Do not hide the pain, we both have scars,
Please, step by step,
Meet me in the middle.

Reckless Drivers

You are driving too fast,
You are driving reckless,
You are not afraid to die,
You are already dead,
A corpse pretending to stay alive.
You are driving yourself
To the inevitable meltdown.
Stop the damn car, let me out!!!!

Bonfire Sessions

You used to sit there and watch
Now you are gone,
I am taking over your throne,
I am watching all lifetimes evaporate
Through the bonfire of our chaos.

Bleeding Out The Time

Do you know how to deck the cards
When you do not like the hand
You were dealt with?
Do you know when to fold?
When to stay in game?
When to increase the bets?

It is like a poker game,
You lose and lose.
You keep losing to me,
I keep stripping you,
Veil by veil,
Layer by layer.
I am branding you,
Ruining you for everyone else
But me.

Run, run as fast as you can,
Run for the hills
For all I care.

Time is filling through your mouth,

Last Thoughts Before The Exit   Cathy BLUE

You are choking up,
You are gonna die,
You will not survive.

Stop fighting against the odds,
Your eyes are bleeding out
This lifetime we could have.

Living With A Manipulator

I am not running scared,
I had survived the worst,
I got my scars to show off
My power, my determination, my strength.

I am not running scared,
I never will.
You left me no safe place,
No home to rest.

Stay and fight it is,
Until I kill you
To stay alive.

Fall To Rise, White

Fall winter fall,
Fall over my frigid soul.
Cover me in snow,
Bury me deep down inside,
Come snowfall,
Be my avalanche,
Take me down,
Bury me 6 feet under and more.
Unleash your magic,
Unleash my magick.

The Crown I Carry

You want what you can not have,
For it is mine,
What shines is mine, mine only.
You are only drawn to it
Like a firefly I wanna put in a jar,
To watch burn bright to die.

My story is mine to write,
I will fight, bleed, take the hit, heal.
I will put all non-believers into shame,
This is my kingdom,
That is my throne,
That is the crown I wear and carry over my head,
Some days heavy like a ton,
Some days all glamour jewels.

If I can not have, I will not want,
All claimed, envy and lust in their eyes,
Starstruck, looking at my golden crown,
Not seeing what it means to carry it,
How alone you actually are,
Nobody can stop bowing whilst talking,
No eye-contact, no honesty.

Last Thoughts Before The Exit   Cathy BLUE

All fake respect, all sugar-coated words.

They look at me and see a queen,
Compared to your radiance, my crown,
Even the sun and moon feel so small,
I am the smallest of them all,
They think I am nothing,
Invisible without my crown.

So be it, bring it on,
I will shatter destiny if need be,
I will slay them all, I can do!
I am the Queen of my own kingdom,
My body, my heart, my soul,
Nobody speaks from a loud tone to me!

I rule this kingdom with an iron fist,
No negotiations, no second chances,
The future shall be sculpted by my will,
Watch me burn down the world today.

Mirror Mirror Of The Soul

Look past the unloved parts of you,
Try to see what they love about you.
Darlin', you had been asking this question
For too long, to the wrong mirrors, muted.

Let me be your mirror,
Ask me about you,
Ask me what I love about you,
I'll tell you all. I will tell you all.

The mirror will talk back,
You ready for that, darlin'?
Did you always assume,
The mirror is picture perfect?

Darlin', you only see
A very well polished surface.
When you look at the mirror,
Do you see the shatters of it?

Darlin', we all have our cracks,

Last Thoughts Before The Exit   Cathy BLUE

Life breaks us all,
Chew us alive then spits out,
Beaten, barely alive.
We are all damaged,
In our own ways.

I'm just a reflection,
You are the fighter,
You are the survivor,
You are the strong one.
You are the one to fight every day,
You are the amazing one,
You are the amazing one,
I love you.

www.ingramcontent.com/pod-product-compliance
Lightning Source LLC
La Vergne TN
LVHW091305190726
843491LV00001B/423